THE HORSE LIBRARY

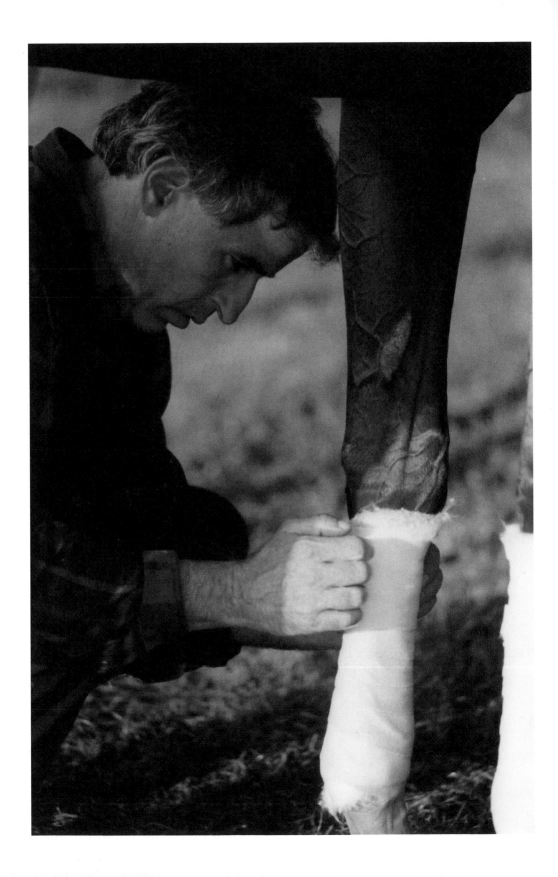

THE HORSE LIBRARY

HORSE CARE AND HEALTH

BRENT KELLEY

CHELSEA HOUSE PUBLISHERS
PHILADELPHIA

Frontis: **A horse's leg may be wrapped to prevent injury when shipping, as well as for therapeutic purposes.**

CHELSEA HOUSE PUBLISHERS

EDITOR IN CHIEF Sally Cheney
ASSOCIATE EDITOR IN CHIEF Kim Shinners
PRODUCTION MANAGER Pamela Loos
ART DIRECTOR Sara Davis

STAFF FOR HORSE CARE AND HEALTH

EDITOR Sally Cheney
ASSOCIATE ART DIRECTOR Takeshi Takahashi
SERIES DESIGNER Keith Trego

CHESTNUT PRODUCTIONS AND CHOPTANK SYNDICATE, INC.

EDITORIAL AND PICTURE RESEARCH Mary Hull and Norman Macht
LAYOUT AND PRODUCTION Lisa Hochstein

http://www.chelseahouse.com

First Printing

1 3 5 7 9 8 6 4 2

Library of Congress Cataloguing-in-Publication Data Applied For.

Horse Library SET: 0-7910-6650-9
Horse Care and Health: 0-7910-6653-3

TABLE OF CONTENTS

This fossil of Mesohippus, a sheep-sized early ancestor of the horse, shows what the animal looked like during the Oligocene era, approximately 25–35 million years ago.

EVOLUTION, FEED, AND SHELTER

Today, the Budweiser Clydesdales are known the world over. They are huge, beautiful animals that eat grasses and grains and work for the benefit of mankind. Their ancient ancestors would never recognize them and would probably be afraid of them if they ever saw them.

The first "horses" appeared 65 to 70 million years ago. They were small, forest-dwelling, browsing creatures about the size of foxes. Gradually, they moved to the open lands and grew—first to the size of sheep, then small ponies, then large ponies, and finally to the size they are today, some even to the size of Clydesdales.

Other changes took place as they evolved. The first horses had four toes on their front feet and three on their rear feet. As they became larger and lived in the open, it became necessary for them to run faster to escape predators. The middle toe took over and the other ones disappeared, remaining today as the splint bones. This enabled them to run faster. Standing only on the middle fingers and toes made them faster.

The pads on the feet of the first horses disappeared as the "toenails" developed into hooves, protecting the single toes that were left. The teeth changed, too. Horses needed to grind the grasses and grains they ate. The side teeth became flatter and slightly ridged so the grass and grain could be sufficiently chewed to release nutrients the horses needed. Today when oats or corn are used for feed, they are usually "cracked" or "crimped" to break the husks on each piece of

Horses Return to the New World

In the early 1600s when the Pilgrims came to New England they brought horses with them, but few survived the trip. The crossings of the North Atlantic were difficult and storms were frequent. Even without storms, however, the rolling motion of the ships on the ocean made it difficult for horses to stand. In attempting to brace themselves, the horses sometimes broke their legs.

Spanish ships generally crossed farther south where the seas were smoother. The horses that survived the crossing to the Americas reproduced and were later used as breeding stock by the colonists.

the grain. This eliminates the possibility of grain passing through the horse undigested; if a horse doesn't actually bite each piece of the grain to break the husk the nutrients within cannot be utilized so cracking or crimping insures that all the grain is available to the horse.

Today's horses still eat grasses and grains, but much of it now is in the forms of hay and prepared feed mixes. Some feeds are now produced in the form of pellets that are highly palatable and digestible.

The original horses developed and began their evolution in the Americas, but they crossed over the land bridge that once existed between Alaska and Siberia, and, over millions of years, migrated throughout the Old World in all directions. Some went south into what is now China and Mongolia; others went west to western Russia and Europe, or southwest to the Arabian peninsula and Africa. None remained in North or South America. They were reintroduced millions of years later by the European explorers.

So, after millions of years, we ended up with tall, fast, beautiful, but still wild animals living in Asia, Europe, and Africa. Early humans hunted them for food and in time they were captured and raised for milk as well as meat.

Then, 4,000 to 6,000 years ago, someone had the idea of hooking horses to the crude early sledges that were pulled by cattle at the time. In Egypt and North Africa, asses were already being used in this manner. When the wheel was finally invented and the sledges became wagons, horses were used to pull them.

One day it occurred to someone to try sitting on a horse. Soon horses became man's most important form of transportation.

All the horses from one area tended to be the same, but they were different from the breeds of other areas. As people moved around in wars or in search of food, horses went with them. Horses from one area were introduced to horses from other areas. Different breeds interbred, developing new breeds of horses.

Eventually man bred horses of one breed with desirable traits to horses of another breed with other desirable traits to see if a horse with the desirable traits of both parents could be produced. In this way, all the breeds we have today were created.

Domestic horses—pets, show horses, racehorses, cow ponies, whatever—must be fed by the people responsible for them. One of the big problems, however, is that many of these people don't feed them correctly.

The biggest mistake is in overfeeding. Horses must be fed according to their needs. Even the largest horse doesn't need grain if it just roams about a field. Good grazing or good quality hay is all an inactive horse needs to remain healthy.

The amount and type of use a horse receives dictates the amount and type of feed the horse requires. For example, a horse ridden once or twice a week needs only a handful or so a day of 10 percent protein feed, but a racehorse in heavy training requires several pounds a day of perhaps 14 percent protein feed.

The danger of overeating is serious. A horse just doesn't seem to know when it has had enough and will eat itself to death. For this reason, the area of grain storage must be inaccessible to the horse. It has to be stored in a closed room to which the horse cannot gain access. In addition, grain must be stored in air-tight containers to protect it from rodents and dampness. Wet grain will mold, which will cause serious health problems in the horse if it is eaten. And rodents will contaminate the food, which can also cause disease in the horse.

Unlike the earliest horses, which were the size of foxes, modern horses, such as the Clydesdale, a draft breed, can grow as tall as 19 hands and up.

Good quality roughage—hay or grazing—is essential. From the spring through the fall good grazing is all that a horse needs; but in most areas hay is necessary in winter. Depending on the horse and the hay, 10 to 30 pounds (about two pounds of hay per 100 pounds of body weight) per day will provide a horse with ample nourishment.

The type of hay is important. It must be of good quality, free of mold and dust. An excellent hay is one consisting of

High-quality, dust-free hay provides essential roughage for horses in winter and in areas where grazing is scarce.

a mixture of timothy grass and clover. A hay called fescue should be avoided at all costs. Fescue should not be used as a pasture grass either because many health problems— from abortions to loss of hooves—are associated with the feeding of this grass. Alfalfa is another hay that is delicious and nutritious, but should not be used because it is simply too high in protein. A horse does not need that level of protein.

Hay should be stored off the ground and out of the weather. Placing it on pallets in a covered shed is one way to maintain it, but it can also be kept in a barn loft or even outside on pallets covered with a canvas tarp. Wet hay will mold quickly and mold is a killer.

It is not necessary to bring a horse inside to feed it. Grain should never be placed directly on the ground, but rather in fence feeders, or hanging buckets, or special ground feeders. Hay may be placed on the ground if you are feeding outdoors, but in a stall there should be a hay rack or hay net so the horse does not damage the hay by walking through it or soiling it in the confined space.

A serious complication of overfeeding grain is laminitis, a condition commonly called founder, in which the hooves separate from the underlying coffin bones. This can result from allowing an overheated horse to drink too much before cooling down. Founder can cause severe pain, and if allowed to continue, can cause the coffin bone to penetrate

 Horse Shelter

A barn is useful but at most times unnecessary. A shed is great except for those situations when a barn is needed. A combination may work best. A shed can easily be built onto a barn. Posts can be placed 12 feet out from the side of a barn and a roof built over that area. This way, a horse will have to spend very little time in the barn and will usually be happier for it. Given a choice, most horses would never go into a stall.

the sole of the foot, leaving the horse unable to walk. Founder is an especially serious problem in ponies. In fact, ponies and fat horses can founder on lush pasture. Once a horse founders, it is necessary to limit its exercise, and it may be necessary to keep it confined to a dry lot and not allow grazing.

Underfeeding is also a problem. This often occurs when the grazing is poor due to drought or winter and not enough supplemental feed is given. If this happens in cold weather, the horse will lose weight rapidly. It was long believed that increasing the amount of hay being fed was the best way to protect the horse in cold weather and keep it warmer, but it is now known that an increase in grain does a better job of protecting a horse's health. Care must be taken, though, to not overdo it.

More important than feed in maintaining a horse's good health is fresh water, which should be available to the horse at all times. An automatic waterer that won't let the water freeze in the winter is ideal, but they are expensive to purchase and install. A water tank is an excellent choice, but must be kept free of ice in the winter, filled at all times, and kept clean. There are safe heaters available for water tanks that keep the water from freezing. They are not expensive and are easy to use.

There are several types of bedding for horses. Straw and wood shavings are the most common. As with hay, straw must be kept dry and mold-free. Proper bedding storage is as important as proper hay storage. Some horses will eat straw bedding, so shavings may be preferable.

The early horses were hardy animals capable of withstanding weather extremes. Some of today's breeds are still able to do that, but most need some protection from the elements. A barn is nice, but not necessary in most situations.

If a barn is available, however, the stalls must be of a size appropriate to the horse's size.

For most full-sized horses, a stall should be 12 feet by 12 feet. A stall for a draft horse—perhaps one of those Clydesdales used by the Budweiser Company—or a foaling stall, should be 12 feet by 14 or 16 feet. For most ponies, 10 feet by 10 feet or 9 feet by 12 feet is sufficient.

Shelter for a pleasure horse can also be a three-sided shed with the fourth side open for the horses to come and go as they please. The size depends on the number of animals that will use it, but 12 feet deep is a good dimension. For two horses, 12 feet by 12 or 16 feet will work unless one of the horses is particularly mean or bossy.

A shed will allow a horse to choose when it wants shelter. Some horses don't mind snow or rain and will be unhappy and make a mess if placed in a stall. With a shed these horses can get shelter if they want it. In extremely hot weather, a shed will also provide shade.

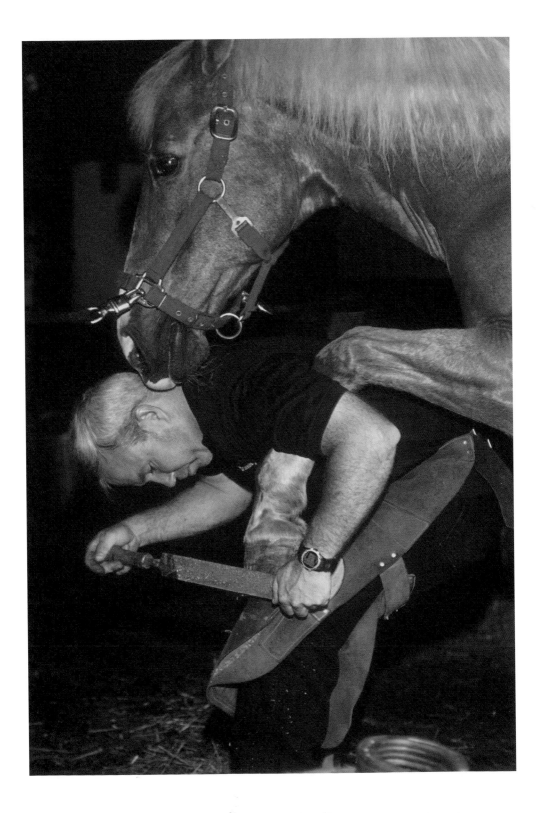

A horse stands quietly while a farrier rasps its front hoof. Like toenails, hooves continue to grow and must be trimmed and filed to stay in good shape.

HORSE HEALTH

There are too many possible horse health and injury problems to cover in one book. When discussing the health of a horse it's important to remember that the veterinarian is the horse's best friend. It is the veterinarian who should be sought to answer any questions about a horse's health or about any injuries that a horse might sustain.

Possibly the horse's worst enemy is tetanus, also called lockjaw, because the disease paralyzes the facial muscles, making it difficult or impossible to swallow. Horses are especially susceptible to this disease, and the problem is compounded by the fact that the causative organism lives in the horse's intestinal tract and is passed in the manure. A horse, therefore, is always in an environment contaminated by tetanus.

Tetanus is transmitted when the organism enters through a puncture wound or other break in the skin. A proper vaccination program with yearly boosters is a must, as is immediate and proper wound care. Thoroughly cleanse any wound, and if it is a puncture, flush it with peroxide. Then call the vet.

Some diseases are spread from horse to horse such as the respiratory conditions known as equine influenza and equine rhinopneumonitis, which are caused by viruses. The symptoms are the same as those for people with upper respiratory infections: fever, cough, and nasal discharge. Rhinopneumonitis can also cause pregnant mares to abort. Vaccination will help to prevent both of these diseases. A proper vaccination program is essential for horses that come in regular contact with other horses at such venues as shows, sales, races, trail rides, and the like. The stress of shipping, combined with the possibility that the other horses at the gathering have not been properly vaccinated, often results in outbreaks of these diseases. Because these diseases are so easily transmitted, bridles and bits must be disinfected after use if they are to be shared by more than one horse.

Strangles, originally called "shipping fever," is a bacterial disease that is easily spread from an infected horse to other horses with which it comes in contact. There is a vaccination for strangles, but it often causes the horse to become ill. For this reason, the decision to vaccinate should be left up to the horse's regular veterinarian who will be aware of the possibilities of the disease occurring in that particular area. Some vets vaccinate only when they know of an outbreak in the immediate vicinity.

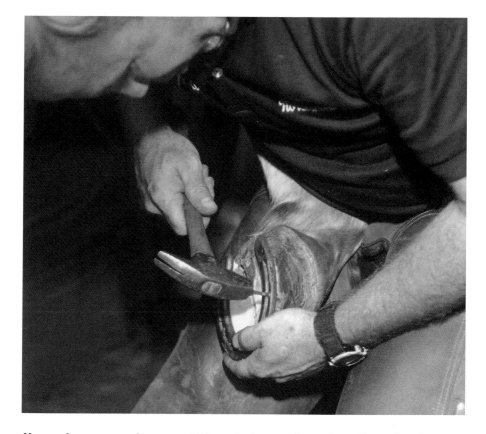

Horseshoes come in many different sizes and can be adjusted to insure a perfect fit; the farrier uses at least eight nails to fasten each shoe.

Equine encephalomyelitis (sleeping sickness) is spread through insect bites. There is a vaccination that is very effective in its prevention, but it requires annual boosters.

Rabies is spread through the saliva of an infected animal, and any warm-blooded animal can get it. It is usually spread when one infected animal bites another, but the disease can also be contracted if the saliva of a rabid animal gets into an open wound. Horses occupy fields that may also be inhabited by foxes, raccoons, and other wild creatures, among whom rabies is a common problem. Therefore, vaccination is essential, and annual boosters must be given.

A horse that gets wet in inclement weather can develop a serious dermatitis —sometimes called "rain scald"—caused by fungal organisms that multiply in the coat. Once this condition takes hold it can take a long time to cure. It can be spread by equipment such as shared blankets, saddles, and halters, so disinfecting or washing equipment is essential to prevent further spread of the fungus.

Equine infectious anemia, or swamp fever, is another disease spread by biting insects, although there is currently no vaccine for its treatment. There is a test for it, however, called the Coggins Test, which is named for the man who devised it. Most places where horses gather require a negative Coggins Test, but all horses should be tested once a year, regardless of their travel schedule. Many states require that the highway patrol stop horse trailers or vans on the road and check to see if the horses have current negative Coggins Tests, so it is necessary to have documentation with the horses. There is no cure, so it is important to know if a horse is infected.

Taking a Horse's Pulse

Using a stethoscope, a horse's pulse may be taken by listening just behind the left elbow. In a resting horse, the pulse rate should be 30 to 40 beats per minute, although there is considerable variation from horse to horse. A pony's normal pulse may be 50, while a draft horse's pulse may be 25. The pulse of some horses may even rise at the sight of a stethoscope.

A pulse higher than 60 in a resting horse indicates that something is wrong with the horse. A pulse above 80 indicates that the horse has serious health problems.

Internal parasites, commonly called worms, are a serious enemy of the horse and can cause weight loss, poor health, and death. The adult parasites live in the intestinal tract of the horse, but immature forms can migrate through internal tissues and enter other organs. A proper deworming program is every bit as important as a proper vaccination program. A horse should be dewormed every two months to insure that the parasite load stays low. The veterinarian will know what products to use to keep a horse as worm-free as possible.

Good records must be kept and checked so a horses's vaccinations and dewormings, as well as hoof and teeth care, are kept on schedule. Any illnesses or injuries and treatments should be recorded.

Horses are frequently wounded. Wounds are possible sources of tetanus or other infection and require prompt attention. All wounds must be thoroughly cleaned; cuts should be sutured by a veterinarian. In the case of a puncture wound, the wound should be flushed with peroxide and a tetanus booster given.

Unattended cuts that leave scars and cuts below the knees and hocks often produce what is called exuberant granulation tissue, or "proud flesh." It is an unsightly lump that continues to grow and will bleed with the slightest bump. Any lesion in these areas must be attended to as soon as possible.

Eye injuries in horses are common because of their poor vision. Such injuries can be caused by low-hanging branches or even such things as bucket hangers. Any eye injury is an emergency and must be seen by the vet as soon as possible.

A horse's hooves, like a person's toenails, grow all the time. Even if the horse doesn't wear shoes, its feet need regular attention. From spring through fall, the hooves grow

You can tell a horse's age by looking at its teeth—a young horse has shallow cups in its incisors. Dishonest horse dealers have been known to drill cups in a horse's teeth in an attempt to make it appear younger.

rapidly and need to be trimmed every month or two, and in the winter they don't grow quite as fast. A broken or cracked hoof can lead to infection or serious lameness, which proper, timely trimming can help prevent.

Gravel, the term used for a common foot problem in horses, is caused by an infection to the sole, or the frog, following an injury. The infection spreads, but because of the anatomy of the foot, (hard hoof on all sides, hard ground below) the infection spreads upward until it reaches a soft spot where it can penetrate to the outer world. This spot is the coronary band (the area between the hoof and the skin of the foot), usually in the front, but also commonly in the heel. The horse gets increasingly lame as the infection moves upward, but relief is almost immediate when it erupts. A one-footed lameness for no apparent reason is usually a gravel. The vet or farrier can often dig it out before it progresses too far.

When a horse wears shoes, its hooves still grow and, in time, its shoes will no longer fit properly and will need to be reset. Horses can also lose or "throw" a shoe, in which case the shoe should be replaced as soon as possible.

Lameness can occur from many causes: minor stone bruises in the sole of the foot, broken bones, and tendon or ligament injuries. Some cases of lameness may be so mild, exhibiting none of the telltale signs, and other cases may be so severe, prohibiting the horse from using the limb entirely. The veterinarian should see any horse afflicted with lameness, even though some lameness is better attended by the blacksmith. The vet will decide who best to treat it.

A horse's feet and ankles are sources of potential health problems. Thrush is an infection occurring in the sulci of the frogs. Thrush comes from standing in unclean, wet conditions for long periods of time. It is one of many reasons why it is important to clean and examine a horse's feet at least once a week, although daily examination is better.

Yet another equine problem that can result from standing in wet conditions is equine pastern dermatitis, also known by names such as scratches, dew poisoning, or grease. This condition is marked by heels and pasterns that develop painful sores.

The horse's teeth, like its feet, continue to grow throughout its life. They grow because the grinding action necessary to chew grain and hay wears the teeth down. As the teeth are ground down they gradually regrow, and sharp points or ridges develop on the edges of the cheek teeth. These points can damage the insides of the cheeks and the tongue if not tended to, and they cause the horse to waste grain. A horse's teeth are tended to by a procedure called floating—rasping the points and ridges away. Most horses require this procedure once a year. A vet should check the horse's teeth every fall and float them if it is necessary. It is possible to determine the age of a horse by looking at the growth of its front teeth.

Colic is one of the most feared conditions that can occur in a horse. Colic is not a disease in itself; it is a collection of signs that show a horse has something wrong internally. The problem is usually associated with the gastrointestinal tract, but not necessarily. The signs of colic include uneasiness, discomfort, straining, kicking at the side, lying down, getting up, rolling, and thrashing. A veterinarian must be called if signs of colic appear, as it can be fatal.

Every horse owner needs a small emergency kit containing a few items that can be used until the vet arrives. Here is a collection that is recommended:

- Nolvasan or other chlorhexidene ointment
- 2-ounce bottle of tincture of iodine
- A small bottle of hydrogen peroxide
- A few sterile gauze pads
- A package of 4 x 4 nonsterile gauze pads
- 2 or 3 rolls of 3-inch Vetwrap or similar bandage

- A pint of liquid disinfectant (Betadine or Nolvasan)
- A small pair of bandage scissors
- A small jar of petroleum jelly
- 5-inch rectal thermometer

A horse's normal body temperature is 99 to 100 degrees Fahrenheit, with a slight variation. If a horse looks and acts sick with a temperature of 100, it is probably sick. If it looks and acts healthy with a temperature of 101, it probably is not sick.

It is a good idea to attach a string to one end of the thermometer and tie a spring clothespin to the other end of the string. To take a horse's temperature, have someone hold the horse for you, then approach it from the left side. Lift the tail or pull it aside. After applying a small amount of petroleum jelly to the thermometer, place it into the rectum about four inches. Clip the clothespin to the tail. This will prevent you from losing the thermometer should the horse expel it, and it will help you to recover the thermometer should it sink all the way into the rectum. To read the temperature, leave the thermometer in place for about two minutes, remove it, and wipe it clean. Record the reading and date on the horse's record.

Many horses enjoy having a bath and playing with the hose spray, especially in hot weather.

OWNING A HORSE

Everything involved with horses and horse ownership seems to be expensive. The expenses begin even before a horse is owned.

The reason most people want a horse is to ride it, so the first thing a prospective horse owner must do is learn to ride properly. There are riding schools and instructors available in all areas, but they vary in quality. Check them out and find the best one, then learn to ride.

When it comes to buying a horse the first considerations should be the costs associated with horse ownership, as well as the responsibilities that come with it. The purchase price is only a drop in the bucket of what a horse will cost over the period of ownership. Continuing costs include grain, hay, bedding, health care, and hoof care.

A horse is a daily responsibility. It must be fed, watered, groomed, and cleaned up after. Feeding must be done on a timely basis. Horses are creatures of habit and expect their feed at about the same time every day.

Do not purchase a horse unless you understand the costs and responsibilities of owning one. An experienced horseperson such as a riding instructor can help you locate a horse. A gentle gelding makes an ideal first horse. Under no circumstances should a stallion be a first horse. A mare, although usually of a reasonable temperament, can be unpredictable when she is in heat—a time, lasting three to seven days and coming every three weeks, when her hormone levels make her receptive to a stallion for mating. Always have a potential horse examined by a veterinarian before you purchase it. If the seller does not want a vet to check the horse, look elsewhere as this person is not being honest with you. The seller should also supply a current negative Coggins Test.

The new horse needs a pasture or a paddock. Two acres per horse is the ideal pasture requirement, but with proper feed and care it can be less. Many horses have been kept satisfactorily in backyards, but some communities have restrictions about owning livestock. Check with your town's zoning and planning boards first to make sure there are no restrictions on keeping livestock. Your pasture must be free of hazards such as farm equipment, children's toys, or trash.

The pasture or paddock must be fenced properly with a horse-safe fence. Barbed wire is not safe fencing for horses. A horse's eyesight is poor and wire can be difficult to see;

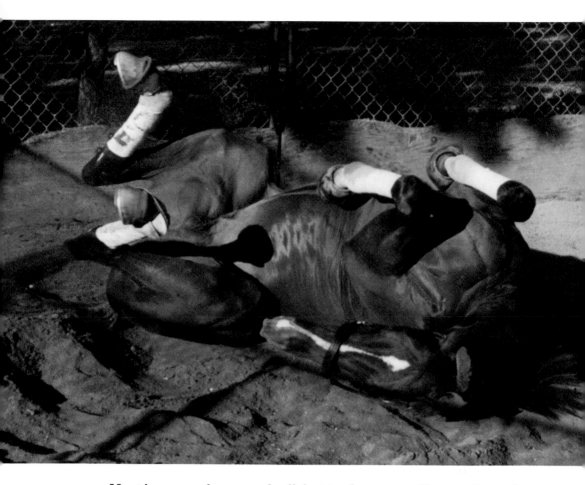

Most horses enjoy a good roll, but too frequent rolling can be a sign of colic.

in addition, a horse's skin is very thin and can easily be cut on barbed wire. Other forms of wire, such as electric fence wire, are not satisfactory unless there is something added to the wire to aid visibility. Woven wire with a top rail makes a good fence. If you don't have a top rail you can tie strips of rags or old towels to the top of the wire every few feet. These will flutter in the wind and help the horse realize there is a fence there. Box wire, commonly called hog wire, or wire livestock fencing, is not a good fence material

Riders who attend horse shows sometimes save a special saddle, like this silver-decorated one, for show, and use a more ordinary one for everyday.

because a horse can accidentally stick a foot or leg through it, causing a serious injury. The best type of fencing for horses is a three- or four-plank wooden fence or split-rail fencing.

Buying the horse is just the beginning. There are many things needed to go along with the horse. Most of the items can be found at a tack shop or feed store, but compare prices before buying. These things will be expensive enough without overspending.

The equipment used on a horse is called tack. The two most important items of tack are a halter and a lead rope, or shank. Without these the horse cannot be properly handled. These two essential pieces of equipment don't have to be fancy, but they must be well made. Halters and lead ropes come in leather, as well as all colors of nylon and rope.

A horse halter must fit properly. Many horses are turned out in the pasture with a halter on, and if the halter does not fit properly the horse can lose it. You don't want to spend hours searching a field for a lost halter. Also, an improperly fitting halter might come off while the horse is being led, and a horse with a very loose halter could hook its foot into the halter while it is lying down. Foals often do this. An adjustable halter will last longer and is recommended.

A halter on a young, growing horse must be checked often. A young horse's head grows but a halter doesn't; if not checked and loosened as needed, the halter will cut into the flesh as the horse grows.

Leather halters and shanks have the big advantage of being able to be cleaned, although they require maintenance to keep them supple and in good shape. Leather tack is also easily repaired if it is broken. Nylon halters come in a wide variety of colors, but they do not clean as well. Unlike leather, though, nylon rarely breaks, which can be an advantage. Rope halters also get dirty easily.

If you are going to show your horse in halter classes, you will want to have a second halter and shank that you can keep clean and use only for show.

For a horse that is to be ridden, a saddle is necessary. Saddles can be very expensive. A used saddle is a more economical option. There are many different types of saddles for different purposes, but for basic riding there are English and Western saddles.

Whatever saddle you choose must fit the horse. The saddle should not rest on the withers but farther back on the horse's back. The best way to fit a saddle is to have an experienced professional do it. Another good way is to try several on the horse. A decent fit can also be found by bending wire coat hangers to the contour of your horse's withers and back. These bent hangers can then be used as templates when choosing a saddle.

There are different types of bridles, but as with saddles the two basic types are English and Western. The basic types of bits are snaffle, straight, and curb. It is important that the bit fit properly. Adjust the straps on the bridle so the bit fits just against the corners of the horse's mouth.

Some people worry about a horse being out in cold weather and they want to put a blanket on it. If your horse has grown a winter coat of hair, then there is no need to use a blanket. As long as the horse has access to shelter when it wants it, it will be fine.

A blanket is needed, however, if you want to show your horse in the winter months and wish to prevent the horse's hair from growing. Without a warm coat of extra hair, the horse has no natural protection against cold and will need a blanket to provide this protection.

A sheet is a lightweight blanket, normally used after a horse has exercised in cool weather. The sheet will allow the horse to stop sweating without being chilled.

In addition to the equipment that a horse wears, there are many other essential items that are used on a horse. Grooming, for example, requires brushes, a currycomb, and a mane comb. The mane comb is pulled through the mane to remove the excess hair. The currycomb is used on the horse's body to remove dirt and dust in the coat. Brushes—a medium one and a soft one—are used after the currycomb to remove surface dust. Brushes may also be used on the legs and face, as a currycomb is too harsh for use on these sensitive areas.

A large sponge is used when bathing a horse, and a sweat scraper is used to remove excess water and sweat from a horse's body.

Electric clippers can be used to remove the long winter coat or to neaten up the fetlocks or roach the mane. A horse usually does not care for the buzzing and the vibration of the clippers, so care must be taken when using them. After a while, most horses will get used to the sound of the clippers, although they will still not like them.

An aid to grooming is a crosstie, which consists of two ropes attached to the walls on either side of a barn aisle or shed. The crossties are snapped to the horse's halter to hold him in place, allowing the groom to have both hands free. A horse must be introduced to crossties carefully because many will fight the restraint at first.

A hoof pick is used to clean mud and dirt from the horse's feet. This should be done often—every day if possible—and always after riding, to make sure your horse doesn't have any stones or pebbles lodged in its hooves.

The Hackamore

The hackamore is a cross between a halter and a bridle. Instead of a bit, it has metal pieces extending down on both sides of the horse's muzzle where the reins are attached. It can be used for both English and Western riding when a horse has a tender or sore mouth, but because the rider has less control over the horse, it should be used only with horses that are well trained.

A hoof tester is an implement that is used to see if a lameness is in the foot. It is similar to a large pair of pliers and is placed from the sole to the hoof wall and squeezed. If there is pain, the horse will react by pulling the foot away, so be careful. It may be necessary to try the testers on several spots to eliminate any possibility of foot lameness.

Other tools and incidentals not used directly on the horse are needed to care for the horse. Buckets and feed tubs are necessary for feed and water in a barn or shed. It is important that they be cleaned regularly; once a week is a good schedule. Plastic is preferable to metal.

Horses make messes and those messes must be cleaned up on a regular basis. Tools needed for cleaning your stall

Stiff body brushes remove dirt, while soft ones are best for use on sensitive areas such as the face and ears. Currycombs help remove dead skin and dust from the horse's coat, and a hoof pick removes dirt and debris from the hooves.

or barn are a pitchfork, a rake, a shovel, and a broom. A muck basket or wheelbarrow is needed to carry the manure away.

If you are planning to show your horse, you will need to be able to transport him from home to the show grounds. Horse trailers come in various sizes, depending on the size and number of horses that will be transported. Cost is dependent on size, amenities, and construction material. There are one-horse trailers and multiple-horse trailers. A roomy trailer will have lots of space for equipment and tack and even sleeping quarters for the horse owner.

After a horse learns to accept a halter and lead rope, it must be taught proper lead manners, such as not to pull on the lead rope or crowd the handler.

EDUCATING
A HORSE

The first horse for a novice rider should be gentle and well broken; but even a well-broken horse sometimes needs to learn new things. The best time to train any horse is from day one—that is, beginning at birth. In a process called imprinting, humans handle newborn foals, establishing familiarity between horse and human as early as possible. At any age, however, repetition, gentleness, and patience are the keys to teaching a horse.

All horses must learn the basics: how to lead, how to stand in crossties, how to have its feet and legs handled and picked up, and, later, how to be ridden or, in some cases, harnessed.

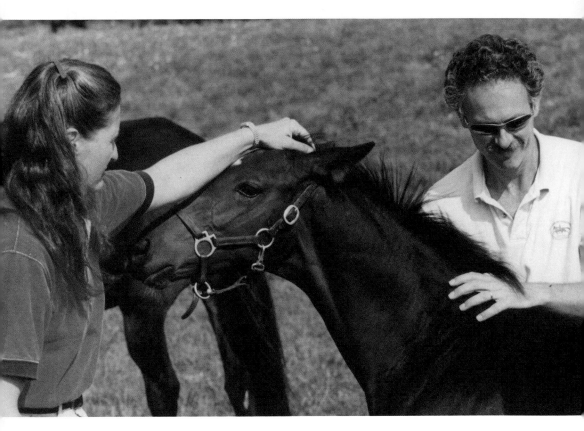

Foals are handled extensively in a process known as imprinting, which accustoms them to humans.

The first three of these are easy if the horse is a young foal. Leading can be taught by putting a halter on and leading the baby while someone else leads the mare. There will be initial pulling and balking; but by staying next to the foal's left shoulder with the shank in the left hand and the right hand on the foal's withers, within a few days the foal will allow itself to be led. After a week or two, the foal will allow itself to be led away from its dam, or mother.

Once the foal is comfortable being led, crosstying is easy, but use only one tie to begin with. When the foal is first attached to the tie, stand by it in the same position as when teaching it to lead. Eventually the foal can be left. Once this step is accepted, try both ties.

Handling the feet is a bit more challenging. Begin by rubbing the foal all over—head, neck, body, belly, and rump. There will be initial disapproval, but repetition will get the foal familiar with being handled. The belly is especially ticklish, but the foal will get used to it once it realizes that it won't hurt.

Once the body can be touched all over—usually a few days—begin rubbing downward on the legs. A second person must be present to hold the foal when this step begins. Kicks—even kicks by small foals—hurt and can do serious damage to a person.

Once the foal allows its legs to be handled all the way to the hooves, the legs can usually be picked up. Squeezing gently just above the pastern will usually cause the foal to lift that leg. Once it is lifted, hold it. The foal's initial response will be to pull away, but be firm. After a few repetitions, picking up the feet will be no problem.

The same steps can be used on an untrained older horse, but the handler must be much more careful. Teaching an older horse to lead is slightly different because there is no mother around for it to follow. The initial teaching can be done in a stall. The handler is positioned the same as with a foal and the horse is maneuvered around the stall several times a day for a few days. Then the horse can be led outside the stall.

Teaching a horse to be ridden—a process commonly called "breaking," but which should more correctly be called "gentling"— is not nearly as difficult as many claim it is. The initial training of leading and body and leg handling have gotten the horse used to being touched and handled, so the next step is to put something on its back. This is always a two-person operation and is always done in a stall or other enclosed area. It should not be done before a horse is at least a year-and-a-half old.

Place a bridle and gentle bit on the horse's head. If the horse is used to having a halter put on and off, the bridle will be accepted as a halter. The bit, although played with and wiggled, will eventually be tolerated.

To get the horse used to wearing something on its back, begin by placing towels or saddlecloths there. With most horses, acceptance will come in a day or two. Next, place a saddle on the horse without cinching it. This will soon be accepted. Then cinch the saddle loosely. After the horse has gotten used to the saddle a few times, gradually cinch the girth a little tighter.

Now is the time for extra weight. With the saddle on and cinched, and one person holding the horse, the other person lies across the saddle on his chest. This should be repeated frequently until the horse accepts the weight. Then it is time to mount, wearing a helmet. By this time there should be minimal resistance. Do this for a few minutes at a time, several times over a period of several days. The person holding the horse should move it about the stall or pen as the horse becomes used to the person on its back. Once the horse is moving easily and comfortably with the person on it, it can be led out of the stall. The rider must be alert to the possibility of anything startling the horse.

Some horses "spook," or jump or shy away, at certain objects. This is a serious problem with some horses, and it is usually because of their poor eyesight. The object may be something as large as a truck or tractor, or as small and seemingly inconsequential as a blowing leaf or a shadow.

This is a tough problem to deal with. If the frightful object is large and identifiable, show it to the horse. Lead

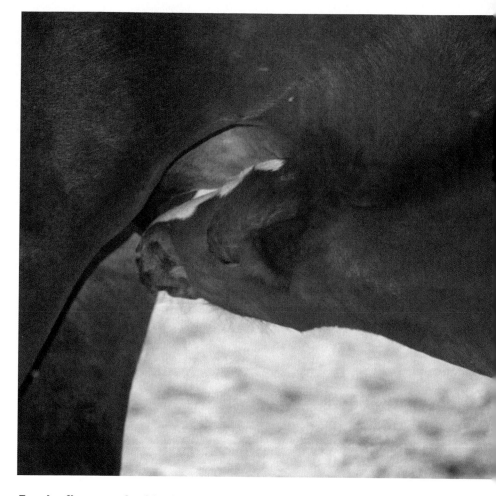

For the first month of its life, a foal gets all its nourishment from its mother's milk, then it is gradually introduced to solid foods.

the horse to the truck or whatever it is and make it stand there by it. Do this a few times and all but the craziest horse will accept and tolerate the object in question.

Shadows, blowing leaves, suddenly-appearing cats, barking dogs, bicycles, and other unpredictable and surprising terrors are much more difficult to handle. A calm, reassuring person, who does not get excited when the horse does, will do wonders for an excited horse. You can also try to accustom

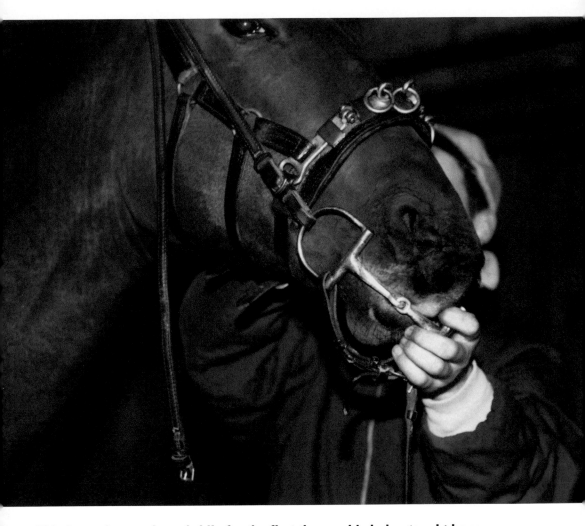

This horse is wearing a bridle for the first time and is being taught how to accept a bit.

your horse to these sights or experiences by repeatedly exposing it to things that excite it. With time, the horse may come to accept these things matter-of-factly.

Even the calmest, most sensible horse, however, will occasionally spook at something strange or unexpected, so a person should always be aware when around horses. The person must always remain calm. Many experienced horsepeople recommend that horse handlers wear shoes or boots with solid or steel toes because a spooky horse, or even a very calm one, can step on a person's feet.

Teaching a horse to load into a trailer can be another challenge. First, all a horse can see is that it's dark in there. It doesn't know what's in store for it inside. Secondly, the way to get into the trailer is not something a horse likes. There are two types of access with trailers. In one, the horse must step up to enter the trailer. This is not something a horse does easily or naturally. Some can be lured in with a bucket of feed and some can be "cradled" in when two people stand on either side of the horse and lock arms behind the horse's rump, then attempt to pull it forward. This method is often quite successful.

Another approach is to place one person in the trailer, holding the horse by the lead rope, while another picks up a front foot and places it on the trailer floor. Once the horse

🐴 What Do You Call That Horse?

A young horse of either sex is called a foal until it is weaned, then it is called a weanling. On the first day of January in the year after its birth, the weanling becomes a yearling. A colt is a male horse younger than five years; a filly is a female horse younger than five years. At age five, a male is called a stallion, and a female is called a mare. A gelding is a male horse of any age that has been castrated. A broodmare is a mare that is used for breeding. A horse's father is called its sire, and its mother is called its dam.

There are many instances when your horse will have to stand still for periods of time, so it is important that he learn to accept being tied up, whether he is between the crossties in the barn or tied to a trailer at a show.

gets used to that, then the other front foot can be picked up and placed alongside the first one. Sometimes this works well on the first try, but usually the horse balks and removes one or both feet. This is really a test of patience, but once the horse has been loaded several times and realizes it has nothing to fear from the trailer, loading should no longer be a problem.

The other type of trailer access is one in which the trailer has a ramp that pulls out, giving the horse a gradual slope into the trailer. This is usually more readily accepted by most horses, but it can also be a problem requiring great patience. The ramp is made of metal and even though there is a rubber mat on it, it is unnatural footing for a horse. When the horse's weight is placed on it, it sags and often makes noise. This makes the inexperienced loading horse back up. When using a ramp, a feed lure, cradling, or the placing of the horse's feet may be tried and often they work. Patience is the key. With time the horse will learn, and once the learning is accomplished, future trailer loading is not a problem.

If the trailer is a multi-horse trailer, loading an experienced loader first will often help inexperienced horses to load. They will follow the horse already on the trailer and learn much more quickly. Even if it is a small, one-horse trailer, loading an experienced loader and then taking it off will sometimes reassure the inexperienced loader. Many times that's all it takes.

Riders and horses line up for inspection by the judge. Preparing for a horse show takes time and lots of hard work, both on and off your horse.

HORSE SHOWS

There is a horse show for everyone. They range from huge national events to small local shows; and from shows with classes for all types of horses to those catering to only one breed or talent. Some last one day or evening, while others last for days. Some have large cash prizes and trophies, and others give only ribbons as awards.

Race meets have been held for several centuries, but horse shows didn't become popular until well into the 1800s. "My horse is faster than your horse," was a common boast in earlier times; but "my horse is prettier than your horse," or "my horse is better trained than your horse," are fairly new ways for the horse owner to show their pride. It wasn't until the 20th century that horse shows became common. The biggest show, the National, held in Madison Square Garden in New York, was first held in 1883. In the following years more shows, large and small, began appearing. In 1917, representatives of about 50 shows from across the country met in New York and organized the American Horse Shows Association (AHSA). Rules and regulations were drawn up so a show in Atlanta would have the same requirements and expectations as a show in Denver or Milwaukee. Preparation could be the same for shows anywhere, and the basis for judging was made uniform.

Not all shows are sanctioned by the AHSA, however. Small local or county shows may be little more than informal gatherings of local people who share a love of horses.

But whether it is a large show in a major city, a Quarter Horse show in the Southwest, or a local show in rural Tennessee, there is much that is the same. All shows have rules, classes, judges, entry fees, and prizes.

What type of show you enter depends on the kind of horse you have and how it has been trained. There are shows for specific breeds, such as Arabians or Quarter Horses, and there are classes within a breed. A three-gaited American Saddlebred, for example, does not show with a five-gaited American Saddlebred.

The main thing horse shows have in common is the extensive preparation of the horse. At any show, the horse is the center of attention, and it must be at its best. It isn't possible to have a horse looking its best simply by bathing and brushing it the day before a show. Conditioning a horse for show is a process that takes long preparation and hard work. A horse cannot be trained overnight. Proper training may take months, even years in some cases.

Behind every ribbon is a lot of showmanship, practice, conditioning, and grooming.

To get your horse ready for show you must groom it daily for weeks beforehand. If it is winter, or if the horse has been turned out for a while, you may need to clip its coat. Bathe the horse several times to get the coat as clean as possible. To put a shine on the coat, many horses are fed a small amount of vegetable oil with their daily grain ration.

The mane and tail require a lot of attention. Different breeds and different uses require different appearances. Five-gaited American Saddlebreds, for instance, have long, flowing manes and tails (they usually wear false tailpieces), while hunters' manes are braided, and Hackneys' tails are docked, or cut short. At draft horse shows, the horses sometimes have elaborately decorated and braided mane and tail, which helps to show off the animals' muscular necks and hindquarters. Braiding takes practice, so all of this has to be planned way ahead.

Your horse's feet need preparation, too. They must be trimmed and shod properly so the feet will be at their best. Different breeds have different needs. Tennessee Walking Horses, for example, have very long hooves, while barrel racing Quarter Horses need short hooves to perform at their best. A Tennessee Walker's long hooves add weight, which in turn adds to the horse's "action"—the height to which the feet are lifted when being shown. Quarter Horses were originally selected for small feet, which enable performance horses like a barrel racer to perform sharp turns easily and safely. Proper hoof preparation may take weeks or longer.

Some local shows are small, one-day affairs where the horse is brought in, shown, and taken home the same day, but many shows require overnight stays by both horse and rider. At these shows a stall is provided, but the exhibitor must bring everything else the horse will need.

 **Ponies**

According to AHSA rules, any horse under 14.2 hands (58 inches) is a "pony." This means that a short Thoroughbred (and they do come this short) is classified as a pony. Many Arabians are ponies.

True ponies—Shetlands, Welsh, etc.—are also shown, but with their own kind. Many pony classes could better be called "short horse" classes. If there is a question about height at a show, there is always a measuring stick available to settle the situation. There have been many disputes over 14.2 hands and 14.2^{1}/4 hands.

The following items are usually taken to a show:

- Grain, hay, and bedding
- Feed and water buckets
- A hay net
- Screw eyes and snaps for hanging buckets
- A hammer, screwdriver, and a few nails (just in case)
- A pitchfork, shovel, rake, and muck basket
- Grooming equipment such as a currycomb, mane comb, hoof pick, and brushes; also a sweat scraper, sponge, and a bucket for washing
- Halter(s) and lead shank(s)
- Saddle(s), bridle(s), bit(s), girth(s), stirrups, and crop(s)
- Leg wraps for shipping
- A head guard and nose guard for shipping
- Mane and tail decorations, if needed, also ribbons and rubber bands for braiding
- Blankets and sheets if the weather is cold, or to help cool a horse after exercise; they also help keep the horse clean and free of dust
- A first-aid kit

The exhibitor will also need to bring a change of clothes, toiletries or other travel items, as well as showing attire. This ranges from fancy riding clothes and headwear to clean jeans and cowboy hats, depending on the type of show.

A horse entered in a show must be accustomed to every imaginable distraction. There will be other horses at the showgrounds, as well as strange sights, sounds, and smells, and there will be people and cars, trucks, and trailers coming and going. If the show is located at a fairgrounds, there may also be amusement park rides, concession stands, and other unfamiliar scenes. A spooky or poorly trained horse

Show attire depends on the type of class you enter. This rider is wearing western gear.

will not be able to handle these distractions, so before you consider showing your horse, make sure he is properly prepared, mentally and physically. Some people like to bring their horse to a show even when they are not competing, to accustom it to the sights and sounds associated with these

This rider is dressed for a saddle seat show.

large gatherings. If you have the opportunity to do this, it will help prepare your horse for its first show.

The horse must be well trained, but the rider must be well trained, too. The horse must do what the rider asks of it, and the rider must be skilled enough to make the horse do what he wants it to do. The horse is being judged, of course, but so is the rider.

There are classes for all levels of skill and experience of both the horse and the rider, so showing is a learning process in itself. The rider feels the tension as the time for a class approaches and must be careful not to pass this tension on to the horse.

The horse is groomed and outfitted. The rider is dressed. Finally the class is called, and horse and rider report to the gate of the show ring.

While any sound horse can be trained to be a good trail horse, there are some breeds, such as mules, that are particularly well suited to long-distance riding.

TRAIL AND ENDURANCE RIDING

Trail riding is an easy, fun way to enjoy time with your horse. But for some riders, trail riding is also a popular and competitive sport.

Trail rides require a sound, sensible, and physically fit horse as well as a rider who is in good physical shape. Unlike horse shows, there are no special requirements of equipment or clothing. The fitness of the horse, however, is of utmost importance. Just as a person could not expect to go from the office to run a cross-country race, a horse should not be expected to leave a paddock and ridden 20 to 100 miles at a set speed on a trail or endurance ride. It takes weeks of training for a horse to be fit enough to compete in a competitive trail ride or an endurance riding competition.

The American Endurance Ride Conference (AERC) is the national governing body of endurance riding in the United States. There are several rules, but two deal specifically with the horses: the horses competing must be at least five years old, and they may not compete while on drugs. (Just like human athletes, horses are sometimes given performance-enhancing drugs.) A horse reaches full maturity at age five and these rules prevent young horses from being abused by overwork, as well as horses of any age from being damaged while under the influence of drugs.

Those interested in competitive trail riding may start with what are referred to as Pleasure Rides. These are non-competitive, untimed rides of 15 to 20 miles. Many riders have limited time or can get away only a few times a year, and they stick with this level.

The next step for those who wish to go on is the Non-Competitive Trail Ride, which is 20 to 25 miles. The main differences between this and the Pleasure Ride are the longer distance and the vetting. A veterinarian is on hand to examine the horses before and after the ride.

Once this level has been tried by both horse and rider, the next step up is the Competitive Trail Ride. The minimum length of these is 25 miles, and they are ridden at a set speed. The veterinary parameters are strict, and the final outcome is graded—that is, there are penalties assessed for riding or veterinary infractions.

The Endurance Ride is the top level. This is a stern test for a fast and fit horse. Endurance Rides range from 40 miles to 100 miles a day, and the distance is covered as quickly as the horse can do it. The welfare of the horse is stressed, and those riders found to be abusing their horses are disqualified. The riders must present their horses to a vet at various intervals, and there are short rest periods along the way so both horse and rider can have a breather. Some Endurance Rides go on for two or three days.

The welfare of the horses is of prime concern in these events. All horses are vetted prior to the ride, 30 minutes after the ride is completed, and during the ride, in the case of longer rides.

The first thing the vet does is measure the horse's pulse for a full minute. Then the vet checks the horse over for "lumps and bumps." Any minor injuries or blemishes that existed before the ride should be listed on the pre-event vet sheet. At the final vet check, new marks will be looked for, such as saddle sores or a bruised mouth. Finally, there is the

What Kind of Horse Is Best for Endurance and Trail Riding?

Any sound horse can be trained to be a good trail horse, but there are some breeds that are especially well suited to the sport of competitive long distance riding. Mules are popular mounts because of their surefootedness, but Arabians, Morgans, Thoroughbreds, and Tennessee Walkers are also popular breeds. In general, horses without too much muscling make better endurance horses because they cool down much more quickly than a heavily muscled horse. The faster a horse cools down, the quicker it can recover from strenuous exercise. In the case of endurance horses, smaller is often better. Some of the most successful endurance horses are under 15.2 hands in height.

Many people are introduced to horses or mules for the first time on an organized trail ride.

"trot up." The rider is asked to lead the horse away from the vet at a trot and then back, to see if the horse is sound. Lameness shows up better at the trot than at the walk.

In addition to competitive trail rides, there are hundreds of non-competitive, just-for-fun organized trail rides all over the country that a rider and horse can join for a few dollars. They cover various distances. Some have overnight campouts. They are not timed, and the only competition is the one that exists between riders as to who thinks the most of his or her horse. Rules are few: Don't pass the leader, don't lag behind, and don't ride off into the sunset—stay with the group.

But the main rule of recreational trail riding is to enjoy the companionship of the other riders and the time you get to spend outdoors with your horse.

Bit—a device placed in a horse's mouth which is used to guide the horse

Blacksmith—a person who works on horses' feet; a blacksmith is also called a farrier

Booster—a follow-up vaccination to improve or increase immunity

Bridle—a piece of tack worn on the horse's head and used to control the horse while riding

Coggins Test—a laboratory test to determine if a horse has equine infectious anemia

Coronary band—the area between the skin and the hoof; this is where hoof growth occurs

Colic—a collection of signs that show a horse is uncomfortable or in pain

Cradle—to push a horse by two people locking arms behind it and pulling it forward

Crop—a small whip used to help train a horse

Crosstie—to tie a horse from both sides, usually with ropes from both sides of a barn aisle or shed

Encephalomyelitis—a viral disease affecting the brain

Elbow—the joint formed by the humerus and the radius/ulna in the forelimb, below the shoulder and above the knee

Equine infectious anemia—"swamp fever"; an incurable viral disease for which the Coggins Test was devised

Equine influenza—a viral disease of the respiratory tract

Equine pastern dermatitis—an infection of the skin of the pastern; results from standing for prolonged periods in moisture

Equine rhinopneumonitis—a viral disease of the respiratory and reproductive tracts

Exuberant granulation tissue—"proud flesh"; a proliferation of tissue that will not fully heal; this is usually found on the lower legs

Farrier—another name for a blacksmith

Fetlock—the horse's ankle

Float—to file a horse's teeth to remove sharp points and edges

Founder—laminitis, a serious inflammation of the feet

Frog—the soft triangular pad of the sole of a horse's foot

Gravel—an abscess of the hoof that travels from the ground to the coronary band

Halter—a piece of tack worn on the horse's head and used to lead the horse

Hand—four inches; the unit of measure of a horse's height

Hay net—a wide-spaced net of rope or nylon used to hang hay for a horse's consumption

Heat—the time when a female animal is ready to be bred; in mares this time lasts for three to seven days and comes every three weeks

Hoof pick—a tool used for cleaning dirt and mud from a horse's foot

Hoof tester—a tool used to check for tender spots in a horse's hoof

Laminitis—founder

Lead shank—a strap or rope that attaches to the halter and is used to lead a horse

Pallet—a small wooden platform used to keep things from contacting the ground

Parasite—an organism that lives in or on another organism

Pastern—the area above the hoof up to the fetlock

Pony—for show purposes, a horse shorter than 14.2 hands; for classification purposes, one of a number of breeds that are small in stature

Rabies—a usually fatal disease of warm-blooded animals, spread in the saliva of infected animals

Rein—the strap from the bit to the rider, which is used to control the horse

Splint bones—the vestiges of the second and fourth toes of prehistoric horses

Strangles—a highly contagious bacterial respiratory disease characterized by swollen lymph nodes

Sulci (singular: sulcus)—the depressions at the sides of the frog

Sweat scraper—a flat metal blade used to remove excess water or sweat from a horse

Tack—collective term for all the equipment used on, or worn, by a horse

Tetanus—a bacterial disease affecting the muscles; also called "lockjaw"

Thrush—a bacterial infection of the frog and sulci

Ball, Michael. *Understanding Equine First Aid: Your Guide to Horse Health Care and Management.* Forestville, California: Eclipse, 1998.

Draper, Allison Stark. *Trail Riding: Have Fun, Be Smart.* New York: Rosen Publishing Group, 2000.

Draper, Judith and Kit Houghton, photographer. *Caring for Your Horse: The Comprehensive Guide to Successful Horse and Pony Care.* New York: Lorenz Books, 2000.

Draper, Judith and Kit Houghton, photographer. *The Book of Horses: An Encyclopedia of Horse Breeds of the World.* New York: Lorenz Books, 2000.

Hill, Cherry and Richard Klimesh, photographer. *Horse Handling and Grooming: A Step-By-Step Photographic Guide to Mastering over 100 Horsekeeping Skills.* Pownal, Vermont: Storey Publishing, 1997.

Mettler, John J., D.V.M. *Horse Sense: A Complete Guide to Horse Selection and Care.* Pownal, Vermont: Storey Publishing, 1989.

INDEX

BRENT KELLEY is an equine veterinarian and writer. He is the author of many books on baseball history. Two books (written under the pen name Grant Kendall) tell about his experiences as a veterinarian. He has also written several books for Chelsea House. He is a columnist for *Thoroughbred Times*, a weekly horse racing and breeding publication. He also writes for *Bourbon Times*, a weekly family newspaper. Brent Kelley has written more than 400 articles for magazines and newspapers. He lives in Paris, Kentucky, with his wife, children, and animals.